How Not to
Become a
Little Old Lady

How Not to Become a Little Old Lady

Mary McHugh

Illustrated by Adrienne Hartman

Andrews McMeel
PUBLISHING®

Andrews McMeel Publishing
a division of Andrews McMeel Universal
1130 Walnut Street, Kansas City, Missouri 64106

www.andrewsmcmeel.com

19 20 21 22 23 WKT 17 16 15 14 13

ISBN: 978-0-7407-7233-7
Library of Congress Control Number: 2007934928

Illustrations copyright © 2002 by Adrienne Hartman

ATTENTION: SCHOOLS AND BUSINESSES
Andrews McMeel books are available at quantity discounts with bulk purchase for educational, business, or sales promotional use. For information, please e-mail the Andrews McMeel Publishing Special Sales Department: specialsales@amuniversal.com.

INTRODUCTION

It's one thing to grow older; it's quite another to wake up one morning and discover that you've turned into your Aunt Florence. What's wrong with Aunt Florence? Well, she hasn't exactly kept up with the times and, what's worse, she won't even try. She turns her back on computers and call-waiting, and she clings to the familiar habits of the past that automatically identify her as a Little Old Lady.

The trouble with letting yourself become a Little Old Lady is that you are missing half the fun of being alive in the twenty-first century. Close your mind to any movie made after 1950, stop listening to music not played by a big band, cling to old friends and refuse to make new ones, and your life will be boring and stale.

I've always found the world a fascinating place, no matter how it changes, and, believe me, it has changed dramatically since I was born. There was no TV when I was a child, and now my grandsons have a satellite dish in Seattle so they can watch the Yankees. I never want to stop learning from people younger than I am. I want to keep on tap-dancing in Macy's annual Tap-a-Thon with six thousand people every August. There is so much going on out there, and I don't want to miss any of it!

Creeping Little Old Lady-hood is everywhere, and every woman is vulnerable. How do you keep it from happening to you? Keep an eye out for the telltale signs.

Little Old Ladies...

. . . have never seen a ladies' room that was clean enough.

. . . save grocery coupons, which
have expired by the time
they try to use them.

. . . think people will be surprised
when they tell them,
"I'm eighty-two years old."

. . . can produce pictures of
their grandchildren before
you get a chance to say hello.

. . . have tightly curled, scrunched-up hair left over from the '40s.

. . . talk about their bowel habits.

. . . consider ice cream a basic
food group.

. . . talk baby-talk to their cats in front of strangers.

. . . still have a photographic
memory—
they've just run out of film.

. . . say, "Everyone tells me I look much younger than I am."

. . . fart in public.

. . . talk about their root canals during lunch.

. . . cover every surface of the living room with little china and glass things that fall over when you walk by them.

. . . don't believe in cholesterol and cook with tons of butter, cream, and eggs.

. . . boil vegetables until they're gray.

. . . start every conversation with a stranger with,
"Where are you from?"
Then they say, "Oh, do you know the Feldmans?"

. . . still expect people to RSVP
when they invite
them to a party.

. . . tell long, boring stories
with no point to them.

. . . believe that there hasn't been any music worth listening to since Frank Sinatra died.

. . . still wear makeup and stockings to the supermarket.

. . . dye their own hair and think nobody can tell.

. . . who live in Florida can't stand "all those old people who are bad drivers."

. . . don't understand why
their grown children don't
return their calls the same day.

. . . remember when
McDonald's hamburgers
cost fifteen cents.

. . . think everybody loves
Regis Philbin.

. . . can rest their breasts on their knees without bending over.

. . . think microwaves fry your brain if you stand near them.

. . . refer to their stomachs
as "tummies."

. . . wonder why a two-pound box
of candy can make them
gain five pounds.

. . . don't know that girdles are now called "shapewear."

. . . who are Catholic still feel
guilty about eating meat
on Friday.

. . . wish Ma Bell would come
back and make the phones
work again.

. . think you're kidding when you
tell them there's a rock
band called
"Post-Surgical Adhesions."

. . . are shocked at the idea of
coed dorms.

. . . think nine dollars is an
outrageous price to pay for
one feature movie and
four previews.

. . . won't wear white shoes
before Memorial Day
or after Labor Day.

. . . try to pass off their liver
spots as large freckles.

. . . can't call people by their
first names unless
they've know them
for ten years.

. . . are always crunching
on little hard candies.

. . . complain about the rain,
young people, music, lunch—
everything!

. . . tell grandchildren stories until everyone's eyes glaze over.

. . . think everyone at their high school reunion looks older and fatter than they do.

. . . haven't heard that nobody wears bright blue eye shadow anymore.

. . . wear sleeveless dresses
long after their arms
have started to flap.

. . . think all Spanish-speaking
Americans should stop
it immediately and
learn English.

. . . never met a fattening dessert
they didn't like.

. . . wear plastic bonnets in the rain.

. . . make creaking noises when
they stand up.

. . . make their dogs wear
sweaters when the Little Old
Lady feels cold.

. . . flick on their signal twenty
blocks before they make
the turn.

. . . think everyone talks more softly now.

. . . have senior moments. Two old ladies have been playing cards together for fifty years. One day, one of them says to the other, "Now don't get mad, but I've forgotten your name. What is it?" The other LOL glares at her for a couple of minutes and then says, "How soon do you need it?"

. . . repeat the same story one hundred times.

. . . turn on the left signal when
they're driving and then
turn right.

. . . don't buy new clothes until
the old ones have fallen apart.

. . . talk about the preparations
for a colonoscopy
during dinner.

. . . carry a complete assortment
of snacks and cleaning
products in their purses.

. . . think you are fascinated
by what they had for
lunch yesterday.

. . . always say, "I didn't sleep a wink last night."

. . . think it's cute to talk about
their "boyfriends."

. . . make annoying noises
unwrapping candy
at the theater.

. . . hold up the whole line at the
supermarket counting
out exact change.

. . . refer to the refrigerator as
the "icebox."

. . . look like they're wearing
seersucker when they
are naked.

. . . love the color blue because
it matches their hair
and their veins.

. . . make Christmas presents
out of empty milk cartons
and toilet paper rolls.

. . . miss Kathie Lee.

. . . think that there are times
when chocolate can solve
all their problems.

. . . iron gift-wrap paper and ribbons and use them again.

. . . make reservations for the
Early Bird Special.

. . . haven't gone to a movie
since *The Sound of Music*.

. . . think their hands will smell like gas if they pump their own.

. . . never chew gum in public.

. . . swim with their entire heads out of the water so their hair won't get wet.

. . . ask their fifty-year-old children if they have to go to the bathroom before they leave the house.

. . . won't drink decaffeinated coffee because they think it's still made with Sanka.

. . . describe their vacations by what they ate.

. . . don't understand why anyone would *pay* for water.

. . . wish long-distance operators could actually find a number.

. . . think all Italians eat spaghetti
and are in the Mafia.

. . . don't believe Rock Hudson
was gay because he was so
macho in *Pillow Talk*
with Doris Day.

. . . still call women over forty
"girls."

. . . take half an hour to divide
up the bill in restaurants when
they have lunch with
their friends.

. . . knit covers for their tissue
boxes and extra rolls of
toilet paper.

. . . wonder whatever happened
to housedresses.

. . . still think their husbands are
always right.

. . . have their hair done once a
week and don't shampoo it
in between.

. . . consider a trip to the doctor
a social event.

. . . find it hard to talk into a
clown's mouth to get
a hamburger.

. . . reuse bread bags.

. . . think "old" is ten years older than whatever age they are.

. . . remember when everyone sat around and stared at the radio when Edgar Bergen and Charlie McCarthy were on.

. . . reminisce about the days when
you could mail a letter
for three cents.

. . . remember song lyrics that rhymed "moon" and "June."

. . . remember when women
cooked every day.

. . . need glasses to find their glasses.

. . . remember when you didn't kiss on the first date.

. . . make you look at all the pictures they took on their trip to Akron, Ohio.

. . . say, "I don't want to complain, but . . ." and then they do.

. . . wear their underpants until the elastic breaks and they fall off.

. . . think nobody should say "vagina" out loud, and they certainly shouldn't write a play about it.

. . . keep cooking deep-fried foods even though their husbands are one hundred pounds overweight.

. . . still iron their husbands' undershorts.

. . . drive 23 mph in a 25 mph zone.

. . . loudly whisper things like, "They're very wealthy, you know," or "He has prostate cancer."

. . . use so much hair spray a tornado couldn't mess their "do."

. . . get common sayings just a little bit wrong: "I wouldn't trust him with a ten-foot pole," or "He's made money hand over heels."

. . . take it personally when
Hawaiians say "Hang loose."

. . . refer to pregnancy as a woman being "in trouble" or "in a family way."

. . . think the wrinkles in their ankles are in their stockings.

. . . think cell phones should
be banned.

. . . don't comb their hair in public—they pat it.

. . . bend over to pick something
up and then try to think
of something else to do
while they're down there.

. . . say, "That's nice, dear,"
when you tell them
your dog died, because
they didn't really hear you.

. . . say "I'll just have one piece,"
and then eat half the
box of candy.

. . . think people who live in California are all hippies or gay.

. . . think therapy is a hoax— you just have to take a good look at yourself.

. . . can't always keep up.
A husband said to his wife,
"Honey, let's go upstairs and
make love," and she said, "I
don't know if I can do both."

. . . wish we could go back to everything being "pleasant."

. . . think gas should still cost
thirty cents a gallon.

. . . think all mothers should stay
home with their children.

. . . are convinced that
manufacturers put the wrong
size on clothing these days
because size six doesn't
fit them anymore.

. . . wonder who that wrinkly old lady in the mirror is.

. . . accuse their husbands of
taking their keys when
they lose them.

. . . keep looking for *The Ed Sullivan Show* on TV.

. . . forget which side of the mall they parked their car on and think someone stole it.

. . . can't understand how somebody can go to a large city by herself and not be raped and murdered.

. . . still think "gay" means cheerful.

. . . think the print in newspapers and books is getting smaller and smaller every year.

. . . have more doctors' phone
numbers than friends
in their address books.

. . . head for the bathroom
at the sound of running water.

. . . think zip codes are just another way to make life more difficult.

. . . wish telephone exchanges
still had lovely names like
Butterfield 8 and Plaza 9.

. . . think they have insomnia when they can't get back to sleep at 4 a.m. after going to bed at 8:30.

. . . have canned goods older than their grandchildren.

. . . should open their windows once in a while to let those twenty-year-old smells out.

. . . think "online" means not using your clothes dryer and that a "floppy" is a sagging body part.

. . . don't understand how they can hang something in their closet for six months and it shrinks two sizes.

. . . think the symptoms of stress—eating too much and impulse buying—are their idea of a perfect day.

. . . know what Victoria's Secret is—
nobody who weighs more
than ninety-seven pounds
or is older than thirty
can fit into their stuff.

. . . are somewhere between the
Age of Consent and the
Age of Collapse.

. . . often start a sentence:
"Now in *my* day . . ."

. . . wish we could go back to a time when the worst thing you could catch from the opposite sex was cooties.

. . . wonder why policemen, doctors, and ministers are so young.

. . . think you can catch cold
by getting your feet wet.

. . . wish that just once someone
would ask for proof when
they request a senior citizen
ticket at the movies or
on a train.